HUNTING

EXCITING AND SAFE OUTDOOR FUN

Alan Walker

A Crabtree Seedlings Book

CRABTREE
Publishing Company
www.crabtreebooks.com

Most Commonly Hunted Animals

Big Game: deer, bear, moose

Small Game: rabbit, groundhog, fox

Forest Birds: pheasant, turkey, grouse

Waterfowl: ducks, geese

Table of Contents

Why Hunt?...............................4

Endangered Animals............10

Today's Firearm Weapons...12

Today's Bow Weapons........18

Gun Safety Tips.................22

Glossary..............................23

Index..................................23

Why Hunt?

Humans have been hunting animals for two million years.

Early humans made hunting **tools** from sticks, sharpened rocks, and bone. Over time, the tools became more **effective** with the discovery of new skills and materials.

Today, people use powerful weapons for hunting game. Game are wild animals that are hunted for food and also for sport.

Sport hunting is hunting animals for **recreation**, not food.

Sport hunters sometimes display the animals they have hunted as **trophies**.

Endangered Animals

People are not allowed to hunt **endangered** or protected animals. Before you hunt, make sure you know which animals are protected.

ENDANGERED:
California condor

ENDANGERED:
Florida panther

Some animals, such as eagles, are no longer on the endangered species list, but they are still protected under federal law.

Today's Firearm Weapons

There are two kinds of long guns used for hunting: the shotgun and the rifle. Each gun has a purpose, and each gun shoots a different kind of **ammunition**.

shotgun shell casing

shotgun shell shot (BBs)

shotgun: fires metal shot from a plastic shell case

rifle: fires a single shell from a metal shell case

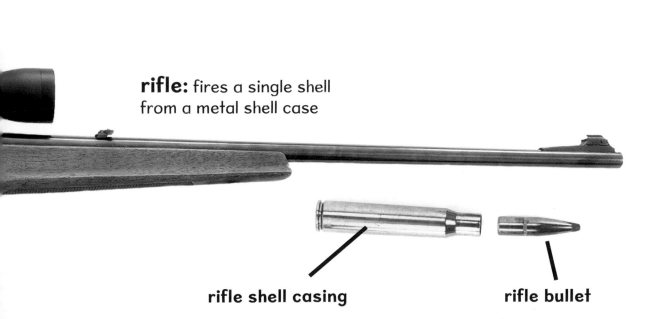

rifle shell casing   **rifle bullet**

Shotguns shoot in a wide pattern. This makes them good for small game, such as grouse.

shotgun shot pattern

Rifles shoot a single shell, leaving a single hole. Rifles are better for hunting big game from a long distance.

rifle shot pattern

Today's Bow Weapons

Bows are much more difficult to hunt with. It takes great skill to track and shoot an animal with a bow.

longbow

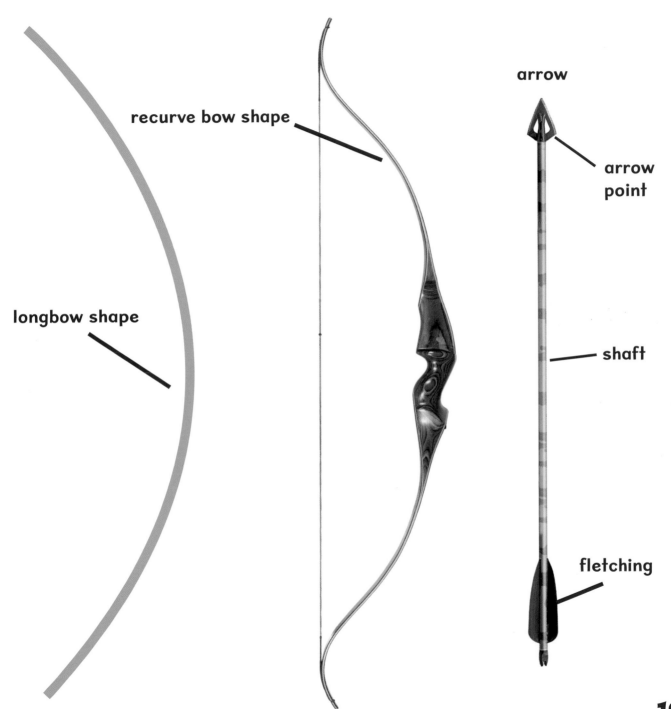

longbow shape

recurve bow shape

arrow

arrow point

shaft

fletching

19

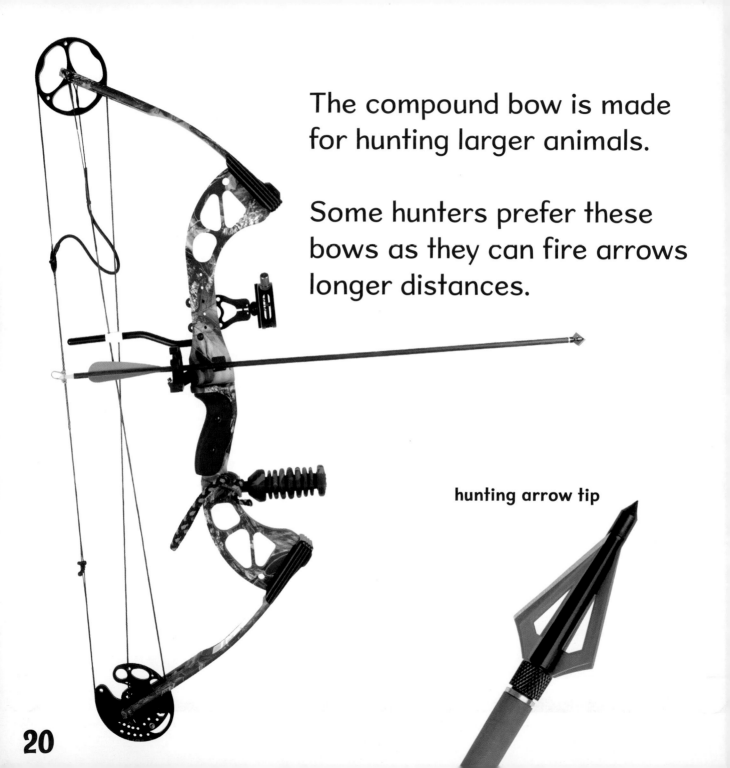

The compound bow is made for hunting larger animals.

Some hunters prefer these bows as they can fire arrows longer distances.

hunting arrow tip

SAFETY NOTE!

Bow hunting can be dangerous. A bow and arrow should never be pointed at or fired toward another person.

GUN SAFETY TIPS

1. Always have a parent or adult with you.

2. NEVER point a gun at anyone—loaded or unloaded.

3. Always have the gun safety on—loaded or unloaded.

4. Never hunt alone.

5. Always wear bright safety clothing, so you can be seen by other hunters.

6. Make sure your barrel is clear before you fire any gun. Never look down the barrel.

7. Never alter or change the weapon in any way.

Wear bright orange clothing and safety glasses.

Wear ear protection, especially on your gun shooting side.

All guns have a safety firing lock. Use it!

Glossary

ammunition (am-yuh-NISH-uhn): Things that can be fired from a weapon, such as bullets or arrows

effective (ih-FEK-tiv): To bring about the proper result

endangered (en-DAYN-jurd): A type of plant or animal that is in danger of becoming extinct

recreation (rek-ree-AY-shuhn): Activities that people do for fun

tools (TOOLZ): Things people use to do different jobs

trophies (TROH-feez): Objects awarded as prizes for victories or successes

Index

ammunition 12
bow(s) 18, 19, 20, 21
rifle(s) 7, 12, 13, 16

safety 7, 21, 22
shotgun(s) 7, 12, 13, 14

School-to-Home Support for Caregivers and Teachers

This book helps children grow by letting them practice reading. Here are a few guiding questions to help the reader build his or her comprehension skills. Possible answers appear here in red.

Before Reading

- **What do I think this book is about?** I think this book is about hunting and why it is a popular sport. I think this book will teach me about gun safety.

- **What do I want to learn about this topic?** I want to learn about how to remain quiet and not scare the animals while hunting. I want to learn what time of day is best to go hunting.

During Reading

- **I wonder why...** I wonder why people enjoy hunting animals for recreation and not for food. I wonder why eagles are no longer on the endangered species list but are still protected from being killed.

- **What have I learned so far?** I have learned that you should always hold your rifle pointed up or pointed down when not firing it. I have learned that some hunters use a bow and arrow to hunt.

After Reading

- **What details did I learn about this topic?** I have learned that a hunter should always wear bright safety clothing, so you can be seen by other hunters. I have learned that all guns have a safety firing lock that should always be on.

- **Read the book again and look for the glossary words.** I see the word *tools* on page 5, and the word *endangered* on page 10. The other glossary words are found on page 23.

Library and Archives Canada Cataloguing in Publication

Available at the Library and Archives Canada

Library of Congress Cataloging-in-Publication Data

Available at the Library of Congress

Crabtree Publishing Company

www.crabtreebooks.com   1–800–387–7650

Print book version produced jointly with Blue Door Education in 2023

Written by: Alan Walker

Print coordinator: Katherine Berti

Printed in the U.S.A./072022/CG20220201

Photo Credits: www.shutterstock.com, www.istock.com COVER, PG 1: shutterstock.com_ LightField Studios. PG 2-3: stock.com_pierluigipalazzi, stock.com_IadSokolovsky, istock.com_Piotr Krzeslak, shutterstock.com_y Tom Franks. PG 4-5: shutterstock.com_Roni Setiawan. PG 6-7: shutterstock.com_Steve Oehlenschlager, shutterstock.com_Just dance. PG 8-9: shutterstock.com_ Jonathan Percy. PG 10-11: istock.com_ gjohnstonphoto, istock.com_jocrebbin, shutterstock.com_escap. PG 12-13: shutterstock.com_ milart, shutterstock.com_Volodymyr Krasyuk, shutterstock.com_Northsweden, shutterstock.com_SolidMaks. PG 14-15: shutterstock.com_Steve Oehlenschlager, istock.com_Nikkisvision, istock.com_Judy_Rothchild. PG 16-17: istock.com_ViktorCap, istock.com_ stsvirkun, istock.com_ReyKamensky. PG18-19: shutterstock.com_Sergei Prokhorov, shutterstock.com_Christian Weber. PG 20-21: shutterstock.com_Keith Publicover, shutterstock.com_Olga Popova, shutterstock.com_ Shane W Thompson. PG 22-23: stock.com_DmitriyKazitsyn, shutterstock.com_Guy J. Sagi, istock.com_Pierdelune.

Published in the United States
Crabtree Publishing
347 Fifth Ave.
Suite 1402-145
New York, NY 10016

Published in Canada
Crabtree Publishing
616 Welland Ave.
St. Catharines, Ontario
L2M 5V6

Important Note: Any sport is safe only when all participants follow rules for safety. Please carefully review the safety tips in this book.